I thought
for my birthday
this would be a go[od]
gift for you. Hope you
like it. I love you.

Ka—.

To Mother With Love

THE HELEN STEINER RICE FOUNDATION

Whatever the celebration, whatever the day, whatever the event, whatever the occasion, Helen Steiner Rice possessed the ability to express the appropriate feeling for that particular moment in time.

A happening became happier, a sentiment more sentimental, a memory more memorable because of her deep sensitivity to put in understandable language the emotion being experienced. Her positive attitude, her concern for others, and her love of God are identifiable threads woven into her life, her works . . . and even her death.

Prior to her passing, she established the HELEN STEINER RICE FOUNDATION, a nonprofit corporation whose purpose is to award grants to worthy charitable programs that aid the elderly, the needy, and the poor. In her lifetime, these were the individuals about whom Mrs. Rice was greatly concerned.

Royalties from the sale of this book will add to the financial capabilities of the HELEN STEINER RICE FOUNDATION, thus making possible additional grants. Each year this foundation presents grants to various, qualified, worthwhile, and charitable programs. Because of her foresight, her caring, and her deep convictions, Helen Steiner Rice continues to touch a countless number of lives. Thank you for your assistance in helping to keep Helen's dream alive.

Virginia J. Ruehlmann, Administrator
The Helen Steiner Rice Foundation
Suite 2100, Atrium Two
221 E. Fourth Street
Cincinnati, Ohio 45201

To Mother With Love

Helen Steiner Rice

Compiled by Virginia J. Ruehlmann

Fleming H. Revell
A Division of Baker Book House Co
Grand Rapids, Michigan 49516

Jacket and interior illustrations by Marcy L. Dilg.

Copyright © 1991 by Virginia J. Ruehlmann
and the Helen Steiner Rice Foundation
Published by Fleming H. Revell
a division of Baker Book House Company
P.O. Box 6287, Grand Rapids, Michigan 49516-6287

ISBN: 0-8007-1649-3

Eighth printing, April 1995

Printed in the United States of America

Dedicated to my mother
with love

Contents

Foreword

Mothers come in numerous shapes, colors, and sizes, various ages and stages of life. They have hair of black, brown, red, blonde, or silver and eyes of different colors and hues.

I remember my mother most, not for her physical characteristics, but for qualities that include her tenderness, her gentleness, her kindnesses to others, her sense of humor, her smile, her willingness to help, her standard of discipline, her unconditional love, her forgiveness, her ability to celebrate life, her gift of sharing, her talent for establishing family traditions, her skill to create something lovely from nothing, and her incredible faith.

With heartfelt nostalgia, I recall Mom on cold, snowy days, giving warm hats and gloves to passing schoolchildren who had none; on hot summer days, handing bottles of homemade lemonade to the work crew repairing our street; on balmy spring days, taking lilacs to the elderly lady two houses away; on crisp autumn days, gathering vibrant colored leaves and ironing them between waxed paper for school projects.

Hers was a heritage learned while she was growing up and never forgotten while growing older in years but younger in thoughts. Memories of my mother cling to my heart, soul, and mind.

Helen Steiner Rice also shared a very special relationship with her mother. Many of her poems were written to, about, or for her mother.

May this compilation of Helen Steiner Rice poems jingle your memory bank and assist you in reliving past moments shared with your mother or appreciating the present times that you are still sharing as precious and valuable experiences.

May mothers everywhere enjoy this collection.

Virginia J. Ruehlmann

Mother

In all this world through all of time
There could not be another
Who could fulfill God's purpose
As completely as a mother!

Mother's Love: A Many-Splendored Miracle

A Mother's Love

A mother's love is something
   that no one can explain,
It is made of deep devotion
   and of sacrifice and pain.
It is endless and unselfish
   and enduring come what may
For nothing can destroy it
   or take that love away.
It is patient and forgiving
   when all others are forsaking,
And it never fails or falters
   even though the heart is breaking.
It believes beyond believing
   when the world around condemns,
And it glows with all the beauty
   of the rarest, brightest gems.
It is far beyond defining,
   it defies all explanation,
And it still remains a secret
   like the mysteries of creation.
A many-splendored miracle
   man cannot understand
And another wondrous evidence
   of God's tender guiding hand.

Love: God's Gift Divine

Love is enduring
And patient and kind,
It judges all things
With the heart not the mind,
And love can transform
The most commonplace
Into beauty and splendor
And sweetness and grace.
For love is unselfish,
Giving more than it takes,
And no matter what happens
Love never forsakes.
It's faithful and trusting
And always believing,
Guileless and honest
And never deceiving.
Yes, love is beyond
What man can define,
For love is immortal
And God's gift is divine!

For Mother
on Mother's Day

No other love
Than mother love
Could do the things
Required of
The one to whom
God gives the keeping
Of His wee lambs,
Awake or sleeping.

There is no fear in love, but perfect love casts out fear.
1 John 4:18 RSV

A Mother's Love Is a Haven
in the Storm of Life

A *mother's love* is like an island
In life's ocean vast and wide,
A peaceful, quiet shelter
From the restless, rising tide.

A *mother's love* is like a fortress
And we seek protection there
When the waves of tribulation
Seem to drown us in despair.

A *mother's love* is a sanctuary
Where our souls can find sweet rest
From the struggle and the tension
Of life's fast and futile quest.

A *mother's love* is like a tower
Rising far above the crowd,
And her smile is like the sunshine
Breaking through a threatening cloud.

A *mother's love* is like a beacon
Burning bright with faith and prayer,
And through the changing scenes of life
We can find a haven there.

For *a mother's love* is fashioned
After God's enduring love,
It is endless and unfailing
Like the love of Him above.

For God knew in His great wisdom
That He couldn't be everywhere,
So He put His little children
In a loving mother's care.

No language can express the power and beauty and heroism and majesty of a mother's love. It shrinks not where man cowers, and grows stronger where man faints, and over the wastes of worldly fortune sends the radiance of its quenchless fidelity like a star in heaven.

Edwin H. Chapin

Motherhood

The dearest gifts that heaven holds,
  The very finest, too,
Were made into one pattern
  That was perfect, sweet, and true;
The angels smiled, well-pleased, and said:
  "Compared to all the others,
This pattern is so wonderful
  Let's use it just for mothers!"
And through the years, a mother
  Has been all that's sweet and good
For there's a bit of God and love,
  In all true motherhood.

What Is a Mother?

It takes a mother's love
to make a house a home,
A place to be remembered,
no matter where we roam.
It takes a mother's patience
to bring a child up right,
And her courage and her cheerfulness
to make a dark day bright.
It takes a mother's thoughtfulness
to mend the heart's deep "hurts,"
And her skill and her endurance
to mend little socks and shirts.
It takes a mother's kindness
to forgive us when we err,
To sympathize in trouble
and bow her head in prayer.
It takes a mother's wisdom
to recognize our needs
And to give us reassurance
by her loving words and deeds.

Mother Is a Word Called Love

Mother is a word called love
And all the world is mindful of
The love that's given and shown to others
Is different from the love of mothers.
For mothers play the leading roles
In giving birth to little souls,
For though small souls are heaven-sent
And we realize they're only lent,
It takes a mother's loving hands
And her gentle heart that understands
To mold and shape this little life
And shelter it through storm and strife.
So mothers are a special race
God sent to earth to take His place,
And mother is a lovely name
That even saints are proud to claim.

Love isn't like a reservoir. You'll never drain it dry. It's much more like a natural spring. The longer and the farther it flows, the stronger and the deeper and the clearer it becomes.

Eddie Cantor

Life's Richest Treasure

Life's richest treasure
That money cannot measure
Is a mother's love,
A heart gift from God above.

The Priceless Gift

The priceless gift of life is love,
For with the help of God above
Love can change the human race
And make this world a better place—
For love dissolves all hate and fear
And makes our vision bright and clear
So we can see and rise above
Our pettiness on wings of love.

May Happiness Smile on You

How to Find Happiness
Through the Year

Everybody, everywhere
       seeks happiness, it's true.
But finding it and keeping it
       seem difficult to do.
Difficult because we think
       that happiness is found
Only in the places where
       wealth and fame abound—
And so we go on searching
       in palaces of pleasure,
Seeking recognition
       and monetary treasure.
Unaware that happiness
       is just a state of mind
Within the reach of everyone
       who takes time to be kind—
For in making others happy
       we will be happy, too
For the happiness you give away
       returns to shine on you.

The woman's task is not easy—no task worth doing is easy—but in doing it, and when she has done it, there shall come to her the highest and holiest joy known to mankind; and having done it, she shall have the reward prophesied in Scripture; for her husband and her children, yes, and all people who realize that her work lies at the foundation of all national happiness and greatness, shall rise up and call her blessed.

Theodore Roosevelt

Everyone Needs Someone

Everyone needs someone
    to be thankful for
And each day of life
    we are aware of this more
For the joy of enjoying
    and the fullness of living
Are found in the hearts of mothers
    that are filled with thanksgiving!

A Sure Way to a Happy Day

Happiness is something
    we create in our mind,
It's not something you search for
    and so seldom find—
It's just waking up
    and beginning the day
By counting our blessings
    and kneeling to pray—
It's giving up thoughts
    that breed discontent
And accepting what comes
    as a gift heaven-sent—
It's giving up wishing
    for things we have not
And making the best of
    whatever we've got—
It's knowing that life
    is determined for us,
And pursuing our tasks
    without fret, fume, or fuss—
For it's by completing
    what God gives us to do
That we find real contentment
    and happiness, too.

Be of Good Cheer

Since fear and dread and worry
Cannot help in any way,
It's much healthier and happier
To be cheerful every day—
And if we'll only try it
We will find, without a doubt,
A cheerful attitude's something
No one should be without—
For when the heart is cheerful
It cannot be filled with fear,
And without fear the way ahead
Seems more distinct and clear—
And we realize there's nothing
We need ever face alone,
For our Heavenly Father loves us
And our problems are His own.

Happiness is like manna; it is to be gathered in grains, and enjoyed every day. It will not keep; it cannot be accumulated; nor have we got to go out of ourselves or into remote places to gather it, since it has rained down from Heaven, at our very doors.

Tryon Edwards

There's Sunshine in a Smile

Life is a mixture
    of sunshine and rain,
Laughter and pleasure,
    teardrops and pain.
All days can't be bright,
    but it's certainly true,
There was never a cloud
    the sun didn't shine through—
So just keep on smiling
    whatever betide you,
Secure in the knowledge
    God is always beside you.
And you'll find when you smile
    your day will be brighter
And all of your burdens
    will seem so much lighter—
For each time you smile
    you will find it is true
Somebody, somewhere
    will *smile back at you.*
And nothing on earth
    can make life more worthwhile
Than the sunshine and warmth
    of a *beautiful smile.*

Safe in His Care

Now I Lay Me Down to Sleep

I remember so well this prayer I said
Each night as my mother tucked me in bed.
And today this same prayer is still the best way
To sign off with God at the end of the day
And to ask Him your soul to safely keep
As you wearily close tired eyes in sleep,
Feeling content that the Father above
Will hold you secure in His great arms of love . . .
And having His promise that if ere you don't wake
His angels will reach down your sweet soul to take
Is perfect assurance that awake or asleep
God is always right there to tenderly keep
All of His children ever safe in His care
For God's here and He's there and He's
     everywhere.
So into His hands each night as I sleep
I commit my soul for the dear Lord to keep,
Knowing that if my soul should take flight
It will soar to the land where there
     is no night.

Mother's Advice

Sometimes when a light
goes out of our life
and we are left
in darkness
and do not know which way to go,
we must put our hand
into the hand of God
and ask Him to lead us . . .
and if we let our life
become a prayer
until we are strong enough
to stand under the weight
of our own thoughts again,
somehow even the most difficult
hours are bearable.

God, Grant Me . . .

Courage and hope
    for every day,
Faith to guide me
    along my way,
Understanding
    and wisdom, too,
And grace to accept
    what life gives me to do.

The Lord is on my side; I will not fear: what can man do unto me? The Lord taketh my part with them that help me: therefore shall I see my desire upon them that hate me. . . . It is better to trust in the Lord than to put confidence in princes.

Psalm 118:6, 7, 9

In Hours of Discouragement
God Is Our Encouragement

Sometimes we feel uncertain
And unsure of everything,
Afraid to make decisions,
Dreading what the day will bring—
We keep wishing it were possible
To dispel all fear and doubt
And to understand more readily
Just what life is all about—
God has given us the answers
Which too often go unheeded,
But if we search His promises
We'll find everything that's needed
To lift our faltering spirits
And renew our courage, too,
For there's absolutely nothing
Too much for God to do—

For the Lord is our salvation
And our strength in every fight,
Our redeemer and protector,
Our eternal guiding light—
He has promised to sustain us,
He's our refuge from all harms,
And underneath this refuge
Are the everlasting arms—
So cast your burden on Him,
Seek His counsel when distressed,
And go to Him for comfort
When you're lonely and oppressed—
For God is our encouragement
In trouble and in trials,
And in suffering and in sorrow
He will turn our tears to smiles.

Trust God where you cannot trace Him. Do not try to penetrate the cloud He brings over you; rather look to the bow that is on it. The mystery is God's; the promise is yours.

John Macduff

My Daily Prayer

God, be my resting place and my
    protection
In hours of trouble, defeat, and dejection . . .
May I never give way to self-pity and sorrow,
May I always be sure of a better tomorrow,
May I stand undaunted come what may
Secure in the knowledge I have only to pray
And ask my Creator and Father above
To keep me serene in His grace and His love!

A Prayer for Patience

God, teach me to be patient—
Teach me to go slow—
Teach me how to wait on You
When my way I do not know.
Teach me sweet forbearance
When things do not go right
So I remain unruffled
When others grow uptight.
Teach me how to quiet
My racing, rising heart
So I may hear the answer
You are trying to impart.
Teach me to let go, dear God,
And pray undisturbed until
My heart is filled with inner peace
And I learn to know Your will!

Enfolded in His Love

The love of God surrounds us
Like the air we breathe around us—
As near as a heartbeat,
    as close as a prayer,
And whenever we need Him
    He'll always be there!

Cast your burden on the Lord, and he will sustain you. . . .
                    Psalm 55:22 RSV

Whenever I'm Discouraged

Whenever I'm discouraged and lost in deep despair
I bundle all my troubles up and go to God in prayer
But there are many, many times He seems so far away
I cannot help but wonder if He hears me when I pray.
Then I beseech Him earnestly to hear my humble plea
And tell me how to serve Him and to do it gallantly
And so I pray these little prayers and hope that He will
  show me
How I can bring more happiness to all the folks who
  know me
And give me hope and courage—enough for every day
And faith to light the darkness when I stumble on my
  way
And love and understanding—enough to make me kind
So I may judge all people with *my heart and not my mind!*

He Asks So Little
and Gives So Much

What must I do
        to insure peace of mind?
Is the answer I'm seeking,
        too hard to find?
How can I know
        what God wants me to be?
How can I tell
        what's expected of me?
Where can I go
        for guidance and aid
To help me correct
        the errors I've made?
The answer is found
        in doing *three things*
And great is the gladness
        that doing them brings . . .
Do justice—Love kindness
        Walk humbly with God—
For with these *three things*
        as your rule and your rod
All things worth having
        are yours to achieve
If you follow God's words
        and have *faith* to *believe!*

Look at that beautiful butterfly, and learn from it to trust God. One might wonder where it could live in tempestuous nights, in the whirlwind, or in the stormy day; but I have noticed it is safe and dry under the broad leaf while rivers have been flooded, and the mountain oaks torn up from their roots.

Jeremy Taylor

Trust and Believe
and You Will Receive

Whatever our problems, troubles, and sorrows,
If we trust in the Lord, there'll be brighter tomorrows,
For there's nothing too much for the great God to do,
And all that He asks or expects from you
Is faith that's unshaken by tribulations and tears
That keeps growing stronger along with the years,
Content in the knowledge that God knows best
And that trouble and sorrow are only a test—
For without God's testing of our soul
It never would reach its ultimate goal . . .
So keep on believing, whatever betide you,
Knowing that God will be with you to guide you,
And all that He promised will be yours to receive
If you trust Him completely and always believe.

Giving Yourself Away

For One Who Gives
So Much to Others

It's not the things that can be bought
    that are life's richest treasure,
It's just the little heart gifts
    that money cannot measure . . .
A cheerful smile, a friendly word,
    a sympathetic nod
Are priceless little treasures
    from the storehouse of our God . . .
They are the things that can't be bought
    with silver or with gold,
For thoughtfulness and kindness
    and love are never sold . . .
They are the priceless things in life
    for which no one can pay,
And the giver finds rich recompense
    in *giving them away*.
And who on earth gives more away
    and does more good for others
Than understanding, kind and wise
    and selfless, loving *mothers*
Who ask no more than just the joy
    of helping those they love
To find in life the happiness
    that they are dreaming of.

"Flowers Leave Their Fragrance on the Hand That Bestows Them"

This old Chinese proverb,
   if practiced each day,
Would change the whole world
   in a wonderful way—
Its truth is so simple,
   it's so easy to do,
And it works every time
   and successfully, too—
For you can't do a kindness
   without a reward,
Not in silver nor gold
   but in joy from the Lord—
You can't light a candle
   to show others the way
Without feeling the warmth
   of that bright little ray—

And you can't pluck a rose,
		all fragrant with dew,
Without part of its fragrance
		remaining with you.

And whose hands bestow
		more fragrant bouquets
Than Mother who daily
		speaks kind words of praise,
A mother whose courage
		and comfort and cheer
Lights bright little candles
		in hearts through the year—
No wonder the hands
		of an unselfish mother
Are symbols of sweetness
		unlike any other.

For the mother is and must be, whether she knows it or not, the greatest, strongest and most lasting teacher her children have. Other influences come and go, but hers is continual; and by the opinion men have of women we can generally judge of the sort of mother they had.

Hannah Whitall Smith

50

The Joy of Unselfish Giving

Time is not measured
    by the years that you live
But by the deeds that you do
    and the joy that you give—
And each day as it comes
    brings a chance to each one
To love to the fullest,
    leaving nothing undone
That would brighten the life
    or lighten the load
Of some weary traveler
    lost on life's road—
So what does it matter
    how long we may live
If as long as we live
    we unselfishly give.

Teach Me

Teach me to give of myself, in whatever way I can, of whatever I have to give. Teach me to value myself, my time, my talents, my purpose, my life, my meaning in Your world.

Love is patient and kind. . . . Love bears all things, believes all things, hopes all things, endures all things.

1 Corinthians 13:4, 7 RSV

Give Lavishly! Live Abundantly!

The more you give, the more you get—
The more you laugh, the less you fret—
The more you do *unselfishly*,
The more you live *abundantly*.

The more of everything you share,
The more you'll always have to spare—
The more you love, the more you'll find
That life is good and friends are kind.

For only *what we give away*,
Enriches us from day to day.

God could not be everywhere, and so He made mothers.

Anonymous

Every Day Is a Reason
for Giving—and Giving
Is the Key to Living!

So let us give ourselves away
Not just today but every day . . .
And remember a kind and thoughtful deed
Or a hand outstretched in time of need
Is the rarest of gifts, for it is a part
Not of the purse but a loving heart—
And he who gives of himself will find
True joy of heart and peace of mind.

Mover of Mountains

Climb Till Your Dream Comes True

Often your tasks will be many,
And more than you think you can do.
Often the road will be rugged
And the hills insurmountable, too.
But always remember,
the hills ahead
Are never as steep as they seem,
And with faith in your heart
start upward
And climb till you reach your dream.
For nothing in life that is worthy
Is ever too hard to achieve
If you have the courage to try it
And you have the faith to believe.
For faith is a force that is greater
Than knowledge or power
or skill
And many defeats turn to triumphs
If you trust in God's wisdom and will.
For faith is a mover of mountains,
There's nothing that God cannot do,
So start out today
with faith in your heart
And climb till your dream comes true!

Ideals Are Like Stars

In this world of casual carelessness
  it's discouraging to try
To keep our morals and standards
  and our ideals high . . .
We are ridiculed and laughed at
  by the smart sophisticate
Who proclaims in brittle banter
  that such things are
  out of date . . .
But no life is worth the living
  unless it's built on truth,
And we lay our life's foundation
  in the golden years of youth . . .
So allow no one to stop you
  or hinder you from laying
A firm and strong foundation
  made of faith and love
  and praying . . .
And remember that ideals
  are like stars up in the sky,
You can never really reach them,
  hanging in the heavens high . . .

But like the mighty mariner
who sailed the storm-tossed sea,
And used the stars to chart
his course
with skill and certainty,
You, too, can chart your course in life
with high ideals and love,
For high ideals are like the stars
that light the sky above . . .
You cannot ever
reach them,
but lift your heart up high
And your life will be as shining
as the stars up in the sky.

The Lord is the strength of his people, he is the saving refuge of
his anointed.

Psalm 28:8 RSV

With God All Things Are Possible!

Nothing is ever too hard to do
If your faith is strong and your purpose is true . . .
So never give up and never stop
Just journey on to the mountaintop!

No man is poor who has had a Godly mother.

Abraham Lincoln

Priceless Treasures

What could I give you that would truly please
In topsy-turvy times like these?
I can't give you freedom from vexations
Or even lessen your irritations
I can't take away or even make less
The things that annoy, disturb, and distress
For stores don't sell a single thing
To make the heart that's troubled sing
They sell the new look suave and bland
But nothing that lends a helping hand,
They sell rare gifts that are ultrasmart
But nothing to warm or comfort the heart
The joys of life that cheer and bless,
The stores don't sell, I must confess
But friends and prayers are priceless treasures
Beyond all monetary measures . . .

And so I say a special prayer
  that God will keep you in His care . . .
And if I can ever help you, dear,
  in any way throughout the year,
You've only to call, for as long as I live
  Such as I have, I freely give!

Hear This Little Prayer

A *Prayer for Those We Love*

"Our Father who art in heaven,"
Hear this little prayer
And reach across the miles today
That stretch from here to there,
So I may feel much closer
To those I'm fondest of
And they may know I think of them
With thankfulness and love,
And help all people everywhere
Who must often dwell apart
To know that they're together
In the haven of the heart!

Lord, Don't Let Me Falter

Oh Lord, don't let me falter—
Don't let me lose my way—
Don't let me cease to carry
My burden, day by day . . .
Oh Lord, don't let me stumble—
Don't let me fall and quit . . .
Oh Lord, please help me find my job
And help me shoulder it.

*I sought the Lord, and he heard me, and delivered me from all
my fears.*

Psalm 34:4

I Said a Little Prayer for You

I said a little prayer for you
    and I asked the Lord above
To keep you safely in His care
    and enfold you in His love
I did not ask for fortune
    for riches or for fame
I only asked for blessings
    in the Savior's holy name
Blessings to surround you
    in times of trial and stress
And inner joy to fill your heart
    with peace and happiness.

All that is purest and best in man is but the echo
of a mother's benediction. The hero's deeds are a
mother's prayers fulfilled.

Frederick W. Morton

A Mother's Day Prayer

Our Father in heaven
  whose love is divine,
Thanks for the love
  of a mother like mine—
And in Thy great mercy
  look down from above
And grant this dear mother
  the gift of Your love—
And all through the year,
  whatever betide her,
Assure her each day
  that You are beside her—
And, Father in heaven,
  show me the way
To lighten her tasks
  and brighten her day,
And bless her dear heart
  with the insight to see
That her love means more
  than the world to me.

In the morning, prayer is the key that opens to us the treasures of God's mercies and blessings; in the evening, it is the key that shuts us up under His protection and safeguard.

Anonymous

At My Mother's Knee

I have worshiped in churches and chapels
I have prayed in the busy street.
I have sought my God and have found Him
Where the waves of the ocean beat.
I have knelt in a silent forest
In the shade of an ancient tree.
But the dearest of all my altars
Was raised at my mother's knee.
God make me the woman of her vision
And purge me of all selfishness
And keep me true to her standards
And help me to live to bless
And then keep me a pilgrim forever
At the shrine of my mother's knee.

Lord, Let Me Serve You

God help me in my feeble way
To somehow do something each day
To show You that I love You best,
And that my faith will stand each test . . .
And let me serve You every day
And feel You near me when I pray . . .
Oh hear my prayer, dear God above,
And make me worthy of Your love.

Begin Each Day
by Kneeling to Pray

Start every day
    with a good morning prayer
And God will bless each thing you do
    and keep you in His care . . .
And never, never sever
    the Spirit's silken strand
That our Father up in heaven
    holds in His mighty hand!

Be careful for nothing; but in every thing by prayer and sup-
plication with thanksgiving let your requests be made known
unto God.

Philippians 4:6

Enjoying Life's Autumn

The Autumn of Life

What a wonderful time is life's autumn
  when the leaves of the trees are all gold,
When God fills each day, as He sends it,
  with memories, priceless and old . . .
What a treasure house filled with rare jewels
  are the blessings of year upon year,
When life has been lived as you've lived it
  in a home where God's presence is dear . . .
And may the deep meaning surrounding this day,
  like the paintbrush of God up above,
Touch your life with wonderful blessings
  and fill your heart brimful with love!

Like a morning dream, life becomes more and more bright the longer we live, and the reason of everything appears more clear. What has puzzled us before seems less mysterious, and the crooked paths look straighter as we approach the end.

Jean Paul Richter

Growing Older
Is Part of God's Plan

You can't hold back the dawn
Or stop the tides from flowing—
Or keep a rose from withering
Or still a wind that's blowing—
And time cannot be halted
in its swift and endless flight
For age is sure to follow youth
like day comes after night . . .
For He who sets our span of years
and watches from above
Replaces youth and beauty
with peace and truth and love . . .
And then our souls are privileged
to see a hidden treasure
That in our youth escaped our eyes
in our pursuit of pleasure . . .
So birthdays are but blessings
that open up the way
To the everlasting beauty
of God's eternal day.

This, Too, Will Pass Away

If I can endure for this minute
Whatever is happening to me,
No matter how heavy my heart is
Or how dark the moment may be—
If I can remain calm and quiet
With all my world crashing about me,
Secure in the knowledge God loves me
When everyone else seems to doubt me—
If I can but keep on believing
What I know in my heart to be true,
That darkness will fade with the morning
And that *this will pass away, too*—
Then nothing in life can defeat me
For as long as this knowledge remains
I can suffer whatever is happening
For I know God will break all the chains
That are binding me tight in *the darkness*
And trying to fill me with fear—
For there is *no night without dawning*
And I know that *my morning* is near.

Slowing Down

My days are so crowded and my hours are
so few . . . and I can no longer work fast
like I used to do . . . but I know I must
learn to be satisfied . . . that God has not
completely denied . . . the joy of working at
a much slower pace . . . for as long as He
gives me a little place . . . to work with
Him in His vineyard of love . . . and to know
that He's helping me from above . . . gives
me strength to meet each day . . . as I
travel along life's changing way!

And I said, This is my infirmity: but I will remember the years of the right hand of the most High. I will remember the works of the Lord: surely I will remember thy wonders of old.

Psalm 77:10, 11

Comfort in Illness

It makes me sad to think of you
Filled with pain and discomfort, too
But I know there's nothing I can do
But talk to the Lord and pray for you.

I wish I could wipe away every trace
Of pain and suffering from your face
But He is *great* and we are small
We just can't alter His will at all.

And none of us would want to try
For more and more, as days go by,
We know His plan for us is best
And He will give us peace and rest.

And earthly pain is never too much
If He has bestowed His merciful touch
And if you look to Him and pray
He will help you through every day.

Just Because You're You

Just Because You're You

May the knowledge that your children
And their sweet children, too
Care for you and love you
Just because you're you
Keep you ever happy
When lonely hours appear
In knowing that their love for you
Is all around you, Mother dear.

Her children rise up and call her blessed.

Proverbs 31:28 RSV

Happy Birthday to My Friend's Mother

I don't know you, that is true
And yet I almost feel I do.
For mothers' hearts are all the same . . .
Regardless of their family name.
And I can't help but feel inside,
How your heart beamed with love and pride,
When your son showed his notes to you
And shared his honors with you, too.
And now that you are eighty-one,
I think the praise your son has won
Is just a bright reflection, dear,
Of the wonderful mother who brought him here.
For children build their lives the way,
Their mothers teach them, day by day.
And all they are and all they do,
They owe to mothers, just like you.

And so today we honor you,
For your faith helped your son to do
The right things, for you made him strong
And taught him what was right and wrong.
Without a mother's love and devotion,
No man would ever win promotion.
You taught him the fundamentals of life,
And placed him then in the hands of his wife.
And together, whatever your son has won,
You both can consider that *you* have done.
So let me bow and salute you, dear,
As you enter into your eighty-first year . . .
To you all credit and honor are due,
And your children's honors belong to you too.
For you live in your children and what they do,
Because they are a part of you.
And here is a wish that our dear God above,
Will bless you today with the gift of His love!

The World Needs
Friendly Folks Like You

In this troubled world
      it's refreshing to find
Someone who still has
      the time to be kind.
Someone who still has
      the faith to believe
That the more you give
      the more you receive.
Someone who's ready
      by thought, word, or deed
To reach out a hand
      in the hour of need.

I think it must somewhere be written that the virtues of mothers shall be visited on their children. . . .

Charles Dickens

To My Favorite Nurse's Mother

You mother every living thing
From poodle dogs to birds that sing.
You give a mother's tender care
To marigolds and maidenhair.
You gently nurture tiny seeds
And help fulfill their growing needs.
You pet and pamper pale tomatoes
And fondle onions and potatoes.
All growing things get your attention
And much, much more than I can mention.
You lend your many loving ways
And spread your sunny little rays
Among God's creatures everywhere
And give them all a mother's care. . . .
So on this day that honors mothers
I honor one who cares for others.
I'm sending my love along with this verse
to the mother of my favorite nurse.

When God thought of Mother, He must have laughed with satisfaction and framed it quickly—so rich, so deep, so divine, so full of soul, power and beauty was the conception.

Henry Ward Beecher

Mother's Day

Mother's Day is remembrance day
And we pause on the path of the year
To pay honor and worshipful tribute
To the mother our heart holds dear . . .
For, whether here or in heaven,
Her love is our haven and guide,
For always the memory of mother
Is a beacon light shining inside . . .
Time cannot destroy her memory
And years can never erase
The tenderness and the beauty
Of the love in a mother's face . . .
And, when we think of our mother,
We draw nearer to God above,
For only God in His greatness
Could fashion a mother's love.

Life's Fairest Flower

I have a garden within my soul
    Of wondrous beauty rare
Wherein the blossoms of all my life
    Bloom ever in splendor fair.

The fragrance and charm of that garden
    Where all of life's flowers bloom,
Fill my aching heart with sweet content,
    And banish failure's gloom.

Each flower a message is bringing,
    A mem'ry of someone dear,
A picture of deepest devotion,
    Dispelling all doubt and fear.

Amid all this beauty and splendor,
    One flower stands forth as queen—
Alone in her dazzling beauty,
    Alone but ever supreme.

This flower of love and devotion,
    Has guided me all thru life,
Softening my grief and my sorrow,
    Sharing my toil and my strife.

This flower has helped me to conquer
      Temptation so black and grim
And led me to victory and honor,
      Over my enemy—sin.

I have vainly sought in my garden,
      Thru blossoms of love and light,
For a flower of equal wonder,
      To compare with this one so bright.

But ever I've met with failure,
      My search has been in vain—
For never a flower existed,
      Like the blossom I can claim.

For after years I now can see,
      Amid life's roses and rue,
God's greatest gift –to a little child,
      My darling mother was you.

Treasuring the Memories

Memories Are a Treasure

Memories are a treasure
    time cannot take away . . .
So may you be surrounded
    by happy ones today . . .
May all the love and tenderness
    of golden years well spent
Come back today to fill your heart
    with beauty and content.

*I remember the days of old; I meditate on all thy works; I muse
on the work of thy hands.*

Psalm 143:5

Deep in My Heart

Happy little memories
Go flitting through my mind
And in all my thoughts and memories
I always seem to find
The picture of your face, Mother
The memory of your touch
And all the other little things
I've come to treasure so much,
You cannot go beyond my thoughts
Or leave my love behind
Because I keep you in my heart
And forever on my mind.

Memories

Precious little memories
Of little things we've done
Make the very darkest day
A bright and happy one.

Tender little memories
Of some word or deed
Give us strength and courage
When we are in need.

Blessed little memories
Help us bear the cross
And soften all the bitterness
Of failure and of loss.

Priceless little memories
Are treasures without price
And through the gateway of the heart
They lead to paradise.

God Needed an Angel

God needed an angel in heaven
So he called my dear mother above
But she's only as far away as my heart
And she lives as before in my love.

*The joys I have possessed are ever mine; out of thy reach, behind
eternity, hid in the sacred treasure of the past, but blest remembrance brings them hourly back.*

John Dryden

Mother Is the Heart of the Home and the Home Is the Heart of Christmas

Memories to treasure are made of Christmas Day,
Made of family gatherings and children as they play . . .

And always it is Mother who plays the leading part
In bringing joy and happiness to each expectant
    heart . . .

These memories grow more meaningful with every
    passing year,
More precious and more beautiful, more treasured and
    more dear . . .

And that is why at Christmastime there comes the
    happy thought
Of all these treasured memories that Mother's love has
    brought . . .

For no one gives more happiness or does more good
    for others
Than understanding, kind and wise and selfless, loving
    mothers . . .

And of all the loving mothers, the dearest one is you,
For you live Christmas every day in every thing you do!

A Mother's Faith

It is a mother's faith
In our Father above
That fills the home with happiness
And the heart with truth and love!